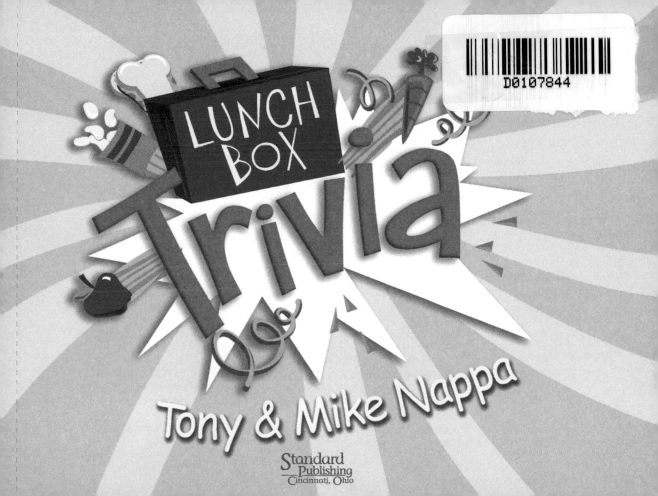

LUNCH BOX
BOX
Trivia

Tony & Mike Nappa

Standard
Publishing
Cincinnati, Ohio

For Brianna, who always asks the best questions.

Standard Publishing, a division of Standex International Corporation, Cincinnati, Ohio.
© 2000 by Nappaland Communications, Inc. All rights reserved.
Bean Sprouts™ and the Bean Sprouts design logo are trademarks of Standard Publishing.
Printed in the United States of America.
Design: Diana Walters. Typesetting: Andrew Quach.

07 06 05 04 03 02 01 00   5 4 3 2 1

ISBN 0-7847-1180-1

Lunch Box Trivia is another creative resource from the authors at Nappaland Communications, Inc.
You can contact the authors through their web site at www.Nappaland.com.

A Note to Parents

I think you should know this book started out as one big joke.

OK, actually, it was a bunch of little jokes that my then nine-year-old son, Tony, and I made up just for fun that really started this thing out. Thanks to Standard Publishing, those jokes (78 to be exact—but who's counting?) were transformed into a family-friendly little tome called *Lunch Box Laughs*. The idea was that you (a parent) could add a bright spot in your child's school day simply by tearing out one of those silly jokes and slipping it into your son or daughter's lunch box.

Well, when we finished that book, Tony and I started brainstorming about other fun things we could give you to pack in a child's lunch. Power tools were quickly crossed off our list (no reliable power source, you know). Hand-held, portable microwave ovens ranked highly—but since no one has invented those yet, we had to move to the next item on our list.

Finally we saw it—silly trivia questions about everything under the sun! After all, God has created this magnificent world, and what are lunch boxes for but to further the exploration of our Creator's genius? (Well, that and to grab a quick bite to eat, of course.)

Think about it. How will your young daughter know if she has arachibutyrophobia unless someone quizzes her on that? And how might your elementary-aged son discover who invented chocolate, or exactly how tall Goliath was, unless the facts are researched during lunch period at school? I see you understand.

Never ones to shirk a challenge, Tony and I spent many hours looking through books in the library and going through all my old theology textbooks from college to gather just the right material for this new book in the *Lunch Box* series. The result was *Lunch Box Trivia: Over 75 Tear-Out Fun Facts About the Bible & Other Cool Stuff*, a book filled with fun and wonderful facts about God, our world, the Bible, science, history, space, and more.

You'll notice that the pages in this book are perforated. That's because we figured the next time you're packing a child's lunch, you might have a sudden urge to tear out a trivia question from this book and slip it in with the juice box and bag of chips.

When your youngster opens lunch at school later that day, he or she will be treated to (we hope) yet another amazing fact that he or she can use to impress friends and teachers alike. And you'll be treated to the satisfaction of knowing you planted a bright spot in your child's day.

Our prayer is that your family will enjoy this book as much as we did. So what are you waiting for? Isn't it time to pack a lunch?

Mike Nappa, 1999

Question:

Which color M&M's® chocolate covered candies will you most frequently find in a one-pound bag of M&M's®?

Answer:

Dark brown, of course! On average, there are about 151 of these in every one-pound bag of M&M's®.

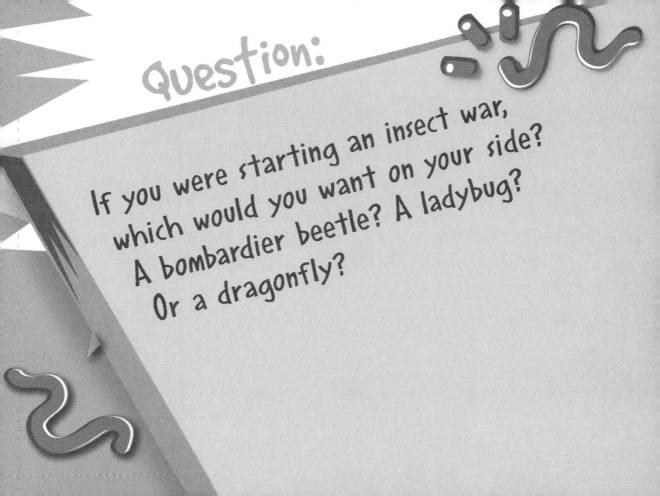

Question:

If you were starting an insect war, which would you want on your side? A bombardier beetle? A ladybug? Or a dragonfly?

The bombardier beetle! If threatened, this little warrior can spray a boiling-hot liquid on attackers, turning away something as small as an ant or as big as a frog!

Question:

It's the best-selling book of all time, and it took 40 people about 1,600 years to write it. What is the name of this awesome book?

Question:

Ever hear of "chicle"? It comes in round shapes, flat shapes, square shapes, thin and fat shapes, and more. Chances are you might have had it in the past week. But what is it? Make your guess now, then check to see if you were right!

Answer:

If you guessed chewing gum, you're right! Chicle is hardened sap from special trees. When flavored and processed, it's made into the gum you and your friends chew!

Question:

The biggest bubble-gum bubble ever blown was bigger than a submarine sandwich (12 inches), but smaller than a large beach ball (36 inches). How big was this world-record bubble?

Answer:

The world's largest bubble-gum bubble was exactly 23 inches wide! Can you blow a bubble that big after school today?

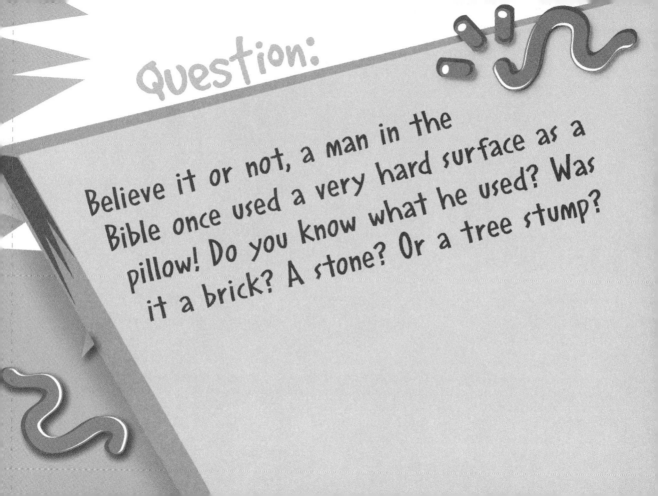

Question:

Believe it or not, a man in the Bible once used a very hard surface as a pillow! Do you know what he used? Was it a brick? A stone? Or a tree stump?

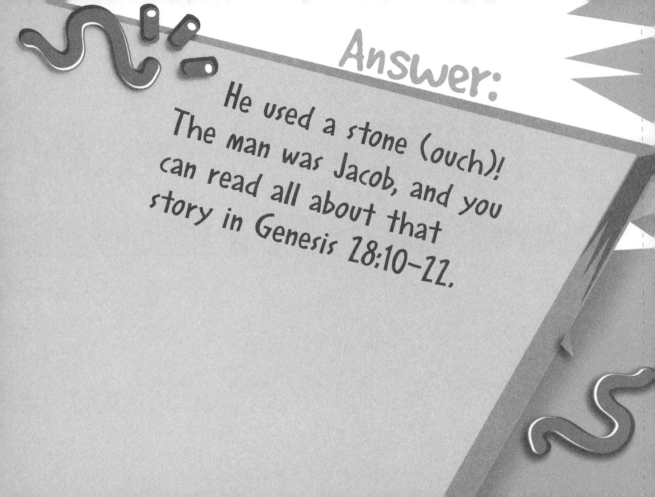

Answer:

He used a stone (ouch)! The man was Jacob, and you can read all about that story in Genesis 28:10–22.

In 1961, a Russian man named Yuri Gagarin flew into outer space. But two creatures from Earth flew in space before any human did. What were they?

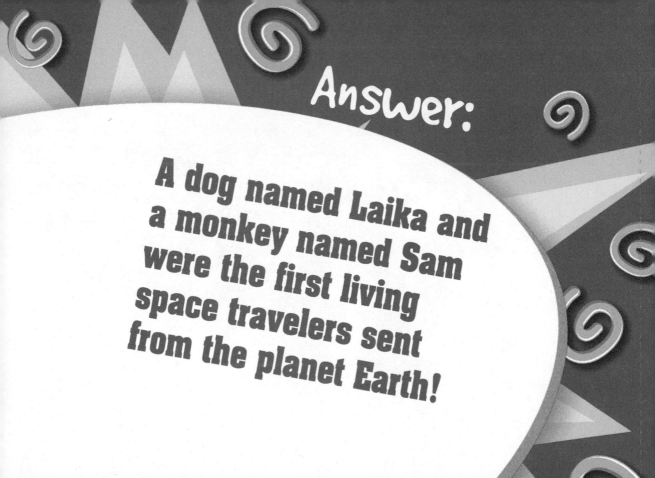

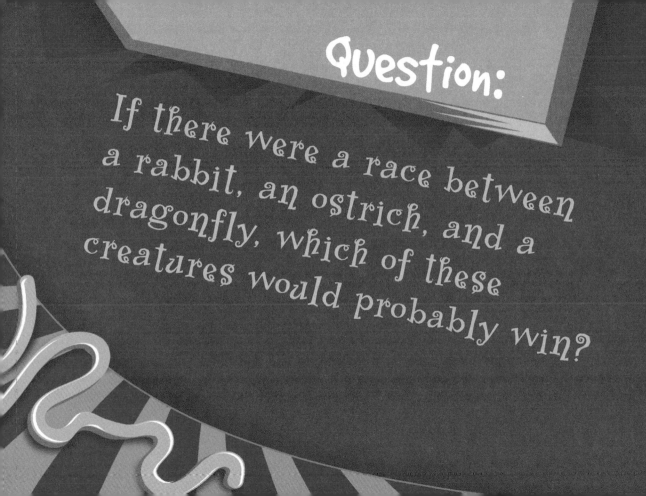

Question:

If there were a race between a rabbit, an ostrich, and a dragonfly, which of these creatures would probably win?

Answer:

The ostrich! This bird can't fly, but it can run at a speed of up to 45 miles per hour—about as fast as a car goes on a major city street. Second place goes to the dragonfly, which can fly at about 36 miles per hour. Running at only 16 miles per hour, our little rabbit comes in last.

Question:

Which is harder, smiling or frowning?

Answer:

Frowning! It takes 43 muscles to frown but only 17 muscles to smile.

Question:

True or False?
At many auctions you can buy a product that's for sale simply by winking.

True! To the auctioneer (the person in charge of the sale), a wink can mean you want to buy the product currently being sold! Scratching or wiggling noses, tipping hats, and tapping ears are other silly ways people tell the auctioneer they want to buy something.

Question:

You probably know that Jesus was born in the city of Bethlehem. But do you know what the word "Bethlehem" means? Is it "house of bread"? "City of angels"? Or "place of miracles"?

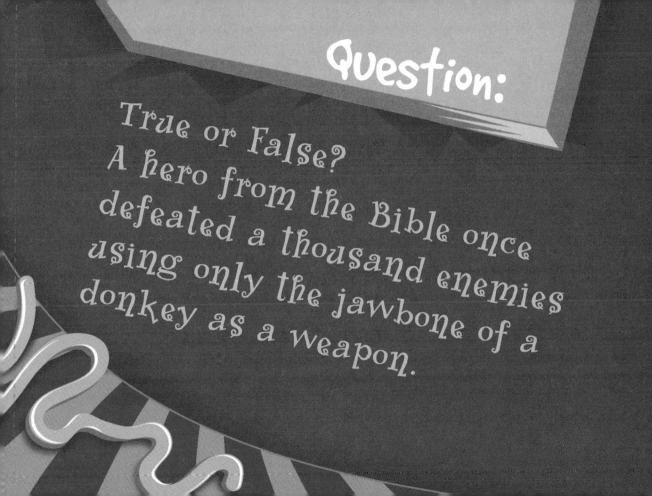

Question:

True or False?
A hero from the Bible once
defeated a thousand enemies
using only the jawbone of a
donkey as a weapon.

Answer:

True! Samson was the one who did it! You can read this story in Judges 15:11-17.

Question:

Hey, all you sports fans!
Did you know that
"20" is the most common
uniform number worn in
all professional sports?
What is the second-most
common number?

Answer:

The second-most common number worn in pro sports is . . . 21.

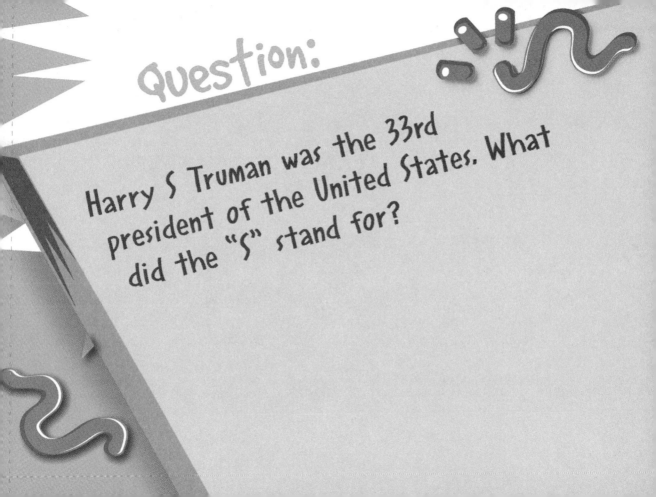

Harry S Truman was the 33rd president of the United States. What did the "S" stand for?

Answer:

The truth is the "S" didn't stand for anything! Harry's parents couldn't agree on a middle name, so they decided to make it "S," which was the first initial of both of Harry's grandfathers.

Question:

True or False?
The Australian archer fish catches the bugs it eats by spitting on them.

True! This creature sucks in a mouthful of water, then spits it out like a tiny water cannon at the bug it wants to eat. That usually knocks the bug into the water where the waiting archer fish can gobble it up!

Question:

King David from the Bible was a mighty warrior who led a mighty army. His archers (the men who shot the bows and arrows) had a special talent. Could they shoot an arrow a thousand feet? Shoot a cherry out of a tree? Or handle their weapons both left- and right-handed?

Answer:

According to 1 Chronicles 12:2, David's men could shoot their arrows both left- and right-handed! Try to write your name using your right hand and then your left hand. You'll see how hard it would be to handle a bow with either hand!

Question:

If this group of people hadn't made chocolate from beans of a cacao plant, it might not exist today! So who invented this sweet treat? Was it the Pennsylvania Dutch? The ancient Egyptians? Or the Aztec Indians of Mexico?

Answer:

The Aztec people of Mexico! In 1519 they shared their creation with Spanish warriors who carried chocolate back to Europe and around the world.

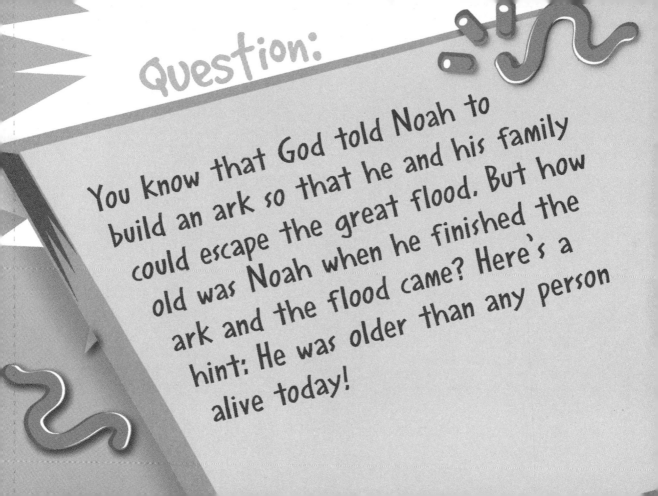

Question:

You know that God told Noah to build an ark so that he and his family could escape the great flood. But how old was Noah when he finished the ark and the flood came? Here's a hint: He was older than any person alive today!

Answer:

Noah was 600 when the flood came and covered the earth! Wow! You can read about Noah and the flood in Genesis 6–8.

Question:

Tootsie Rolls® chocolate candy, Hershey's Kisses® chocolate candy, and Snickers® candy bars are among the top candies eaten by kids today—but which one was created first? Ask three of your friends to guess, then look to see who was right.

The oldest of these candies is the Tootsie Roll®. It was first created more than 100 years ago, in 1896. Hershey's Kisses® came to be in 1907, and the Snickers® bar was invented in 1930.

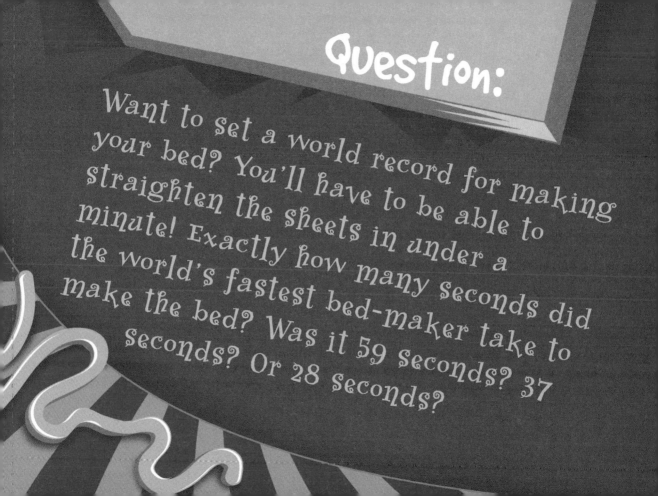

Question:

Want to set a world record for making your bed? You'll have to be able to straighten the sheets in under a minute! Exactly how many seconds did the world's fastest bed-maker take to make the bed? Was it 59 seconds? 37 seconds? Or 28 seconds?

Answer:

The world record for making a bed is 28.2 seconds. Can you beat that? Why not try after school today?

Question:

The Bible tells us that the apostle Paul was a great teacher and Christian missionary. But Paul also worked a different job to earn money for paying his bills. What was Paul's other job? Was he a farmer? A tentmaker? Or a carpenter?

Answer:

According to
Acts 18:3, Paul worked
as a tentmaker.

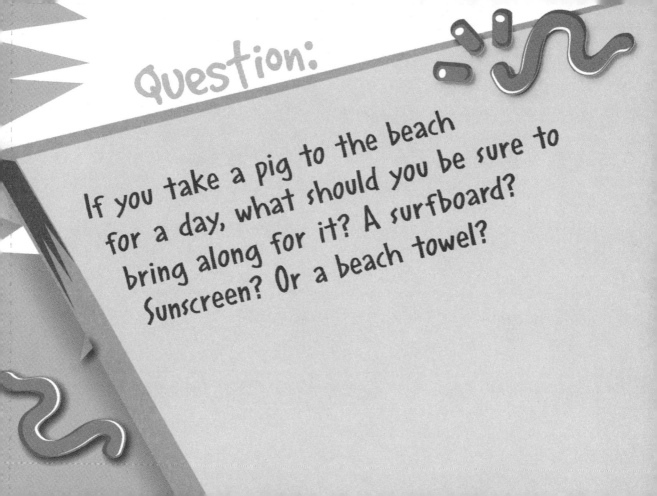

Question:

If you take a pig to the beach for a day, what should you be sure to bring along for it? A surfboard? Sunscreen? Or a beach towel?

Better bring along sunscreen because—like you—your porky little friend could get a sunburn if you don't!

Question:

Everyone knows the planet Earth has one moon in its orbit. But did you know other planets in our solar system have even more? Mars, Jupiter, and Saturn all have more than one moon. Which planet has the most?

If you said Saturn, you're right! With 23 moons in its orbit, this planet has the most of any in our solar system. Jupiter is second, with 16 moons. Mars has only two.

Question:

True or False?
One angel can defeat an
entire army.

Answer:

True! Isaiah 37:36 in the Bible says that one angel defeated 185,000 enemy warriors and stopped them from invading Israel!

Question:

One popular toy in America today actually got its start as a weapon in the 16th century. Was it the jump rope? The hula hoop? Or the yo-yo?

Answer:

The yo-yo! This small modern toy was designed from a weapon used by Philippine warriors during the 1500s. First the warriors would attach a 20-foot rope to a four-pound stone sphere, then "fire" their yo-yos by slinging them at an enemy nearby.

Question:

How much water is really in a watermelon? 50 percent? 75 percent? Or 90 percent? Ask a friend to guess and then check the answer.

A watermelon gets its name for good reason—it's 90 percent water! Tiny cells called "bubble cells" hold the water together so you can eat this sticky, wet, summer treat.

True or False?
Garlic was once so valuable that
people used it to pay taxes.

Answer:

True! People in Siberia during the 17th and 18th centuries paid taxes with garlic.

Question:

Quick! Say your first name out loud right now! How many muscles did you use to say that one word? Here's a hint: It was more than 50, but less than 100.

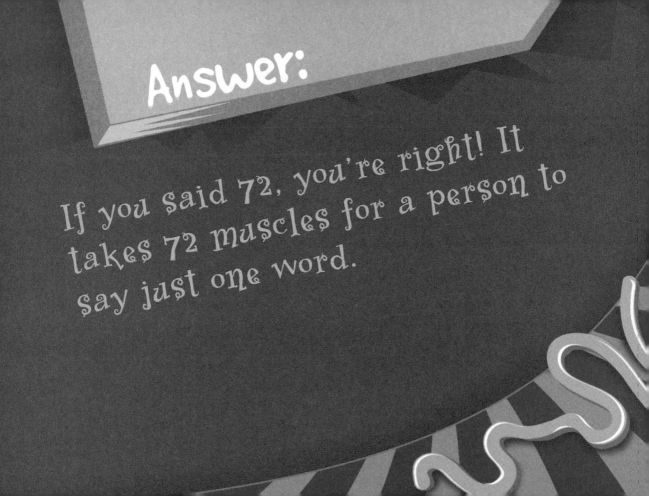

Answer:

If you said 72, you're right! It takes 72 muscles for a person to say just one word.

Question:

You may have learned that the Pacific Ocean is on the west side of the United States, and the Atlantic Ocean is on the east side. But which ocean is bigger?

Answer:

Measuring over 64 million square miles, the Pacific Ocean is not only bigger than the Atlantic, it's the biggest ocean in the whole world! (The Atlantic Ocean is about 33 million square miles.)

Question:

Can you name (in your own words) the first five of the Ten Commandments from the Bible? Here's a hint: The first one is "Don't worship any other gods but God." Now you try the rest!

Exodus 20:3-17 in the Bible tells us that the first five Commandments are

1. Don't worship any other gods but God.
2. Don't make any idols.
3. Don't misuse God's name.
4. Remember the Sabbath day and keep it holy.
5. Respect your mom and dad.

Question:

Can you name (in your own words) the last five of the Ten Commandments from the Bible? Here's a hint: Start with "Don't murder." Now you try the rest!

Answer:

The last five Commandments are
6. Don't murder.
7. Be faithful to your husband or wife.
8. Don't steal.
9. Don't lie.
10. Don't be jealous of things your neighbor has.

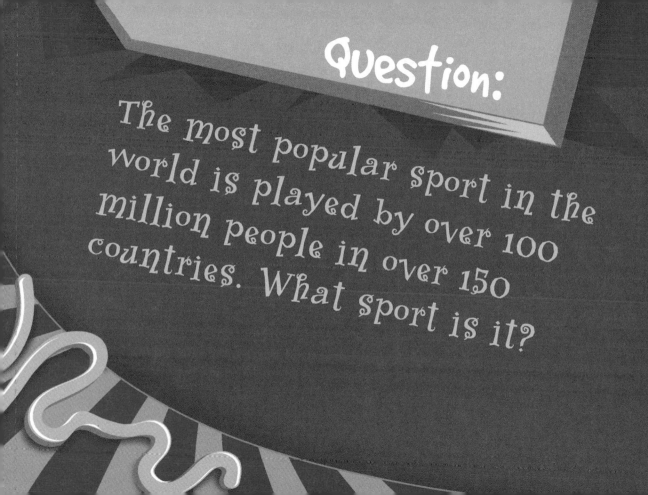

Question:

The most popular sport in the world is played by over 100 million people in over 150 countries. What sport is it?

Answer:

Soccer! (And did you know most people outside the USA call this sport "football"?)

Question:

True or False?
A few hundred years ago, Inca Indians in Peru made common objects like eyebrow tweezers, nails, and plates out of pure gold.

Answer:

True! The Incas thought gold wasn't very valuable at all and so they made everyday objects like eyebrow tweezers, nails, combs, plates, and cups!

If you land on Illinois Avenue while playing the popular board game Monopoly®, should you buy it or save your money for more expensive property?

Buy it! Illinois Avenue is the property that players most often land on while playing the Monopoly® board game. That means you'll get plenty of "rent money" from other players if you own it. (And, in case you're curious, the next best property to own would be B&O Railroad, so be sure to pick that one up, too.)

The Bible tells us that King David was known as a great king and a great warrior. But he was also great at something else. Was it cooking? Making music? Or painting pictures?

The Bible tells us in Amos 6:5 that David was a great musician! In fact, the Bible also suggests that David invented musical instruments that were used to praise God (see I Chronicles 23:5).

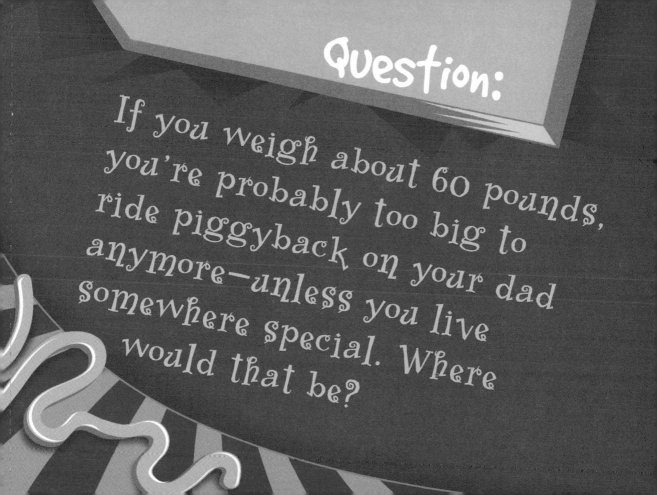

Question:

If you weigh about 60 pounds, you're probably too big to ride piggyback on your dad anymore—unless you live somewhere special. Where would that be?

Answer:

The moon! If you lived on the moon, you would weigh only 10 pounds instead of 60 (one-sixth your normal weight), making it easy for you to hitch a ride on Dad's back again.

Question:

The Bible was not originally written in English. In fact, it was written in three other languages that were later translated into English. Do you know what those languages were? See if you can pick the correct three languages from this list: French, Greek, Spanish, Portuguese, Aramaic, Dutch, Hebrew, Latin.

Answer:

The Bible was originally written in Hebrew, Aramaic, and Greek. Today it has been translated into thousands of languages—including all the languages in the list on the other side of this page!

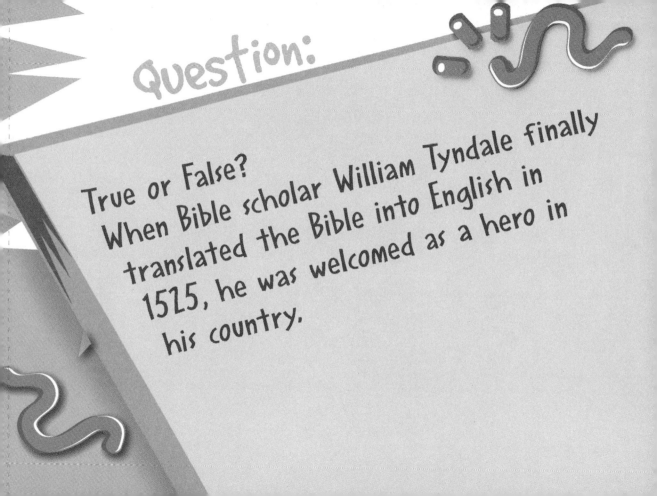

Question:

True or False?
When Bible scholar William Tyndale finally translated the Bible into English in 1525, he was welcomed as a hero in his country.

False! Believe it or not, the King of England branded him a criminal for translating the Bible into English! Tyndale was eventually killed for that "crime." Thankfully, less than a century later, a new king declared it legal to read the Bible in English. (Whew!)

Question:

Ever wonder what doctors 1,000 years ago told their patients to do for headaches? Was it "Chew the bark of a willow tree"? "Take a nap"? Or "Take two aspirin and call me in the morning"?

"Chew the bark of a willow tree!" Willow bark contains a special acid that relieves pain and lowers a fever, so these doctors actually gave good advice!

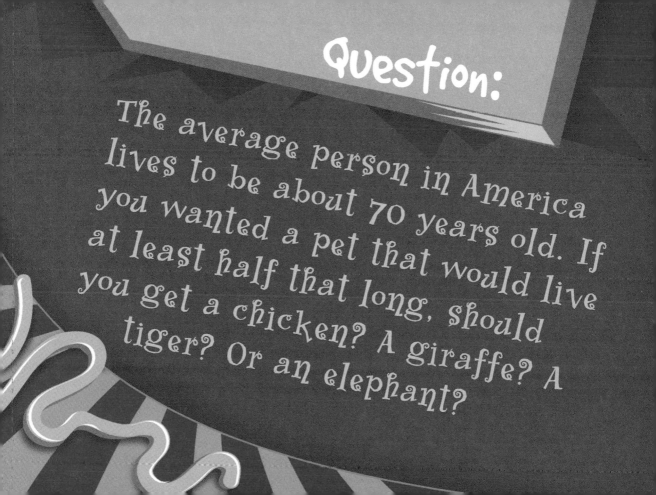

Question:

The average person in America lives to be about 70 years old. If you wanted a pet that would live at least half that long, should you get a chicken? A giraffe? A tiger? Or an elephant?

Answer:

You'd want an elephant! These great animals usually live for about 35 years. A chicken lives only for about seven years, a giraffe about ten years, and a tiger lives about 16 years.

Question:

Some people have intense fears called "phobias." If you have "arachibutyrophobia," what are you afraid of? Is it water? Cafeteria food? Or peanut butter sticking to the roof of your mouth?

Answer:

Arachibutyrophobia is the fear of peanut butter sticking to the roof of your mouth!

Question:

There are 50 states in the United States of America. Which is the biggest?

The largest state in the USA is Alaska! It measures 656,424 square miles. That's big enough to fit the entire state of Texas within Alaska's borders—twice!

Question:

Who is likely to have the most hairs on his or her head? Someone with blond hair? Red hair? Or brown hair?

A person with blond hair typically has the most hairs on his or her head—around 150,000! A brown-haired person usually has about 100,000 hairs. And an average redhead has the least—about 90,000 hairs!

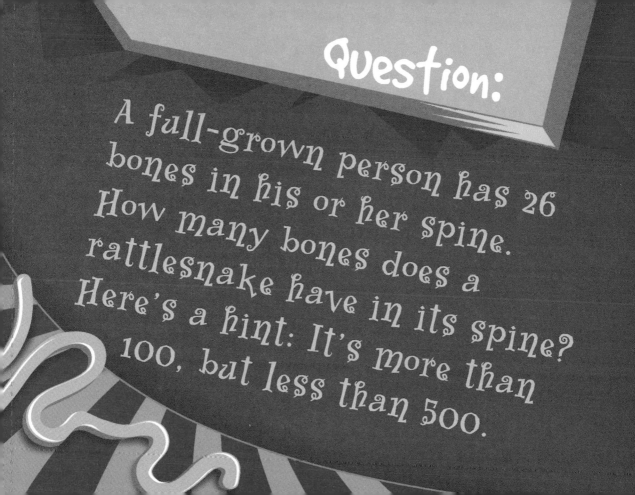

Question:

A full-grown person has 26 bones in his or her spine. How many bones does a rattlesnake have in its spine? Here's a hint: It's more than 100, but less than 500.

Answer:

If you said there are around 200 bones in a rattlesnake spine, you're right! Give yourself a pat on the back for getting this one!

Question:

True or False?
The Bible is not really
one book.

Answer:

True! The Bible is actually a collection of 66 smaller books. There are books on God's law, books of wisdom and poetry, books of history, books of prophecy, books about Jesus' life and the history of the church, and books that were originally letters sent to people and churches.

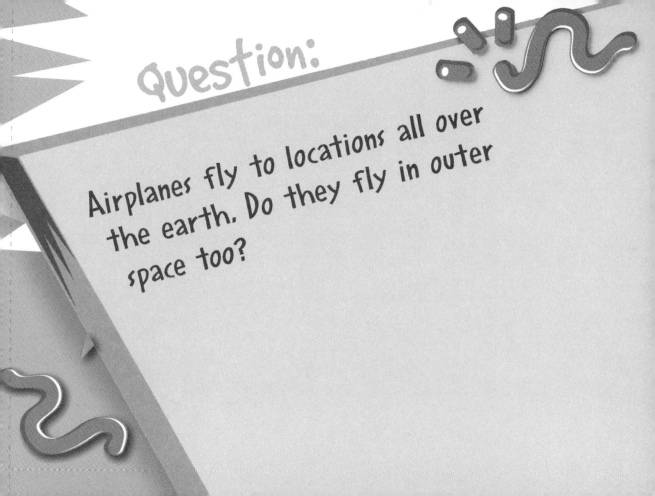

Question:

Airplanes fly to locations all over the earth. Do they fly in outer space too?

No! An airplane flies because it's held up by the streams of air rushing under its wings. There's almost no air in outer space, so an airplane has nothing to hold it up out there!

Question:

Who was the first king of Israel? Was it King David? King Solomon? Or King Saul?

The first king of Israel was King Saul! You can read the story of how he became king in I Samuel chapters 8-11, in the Bible.

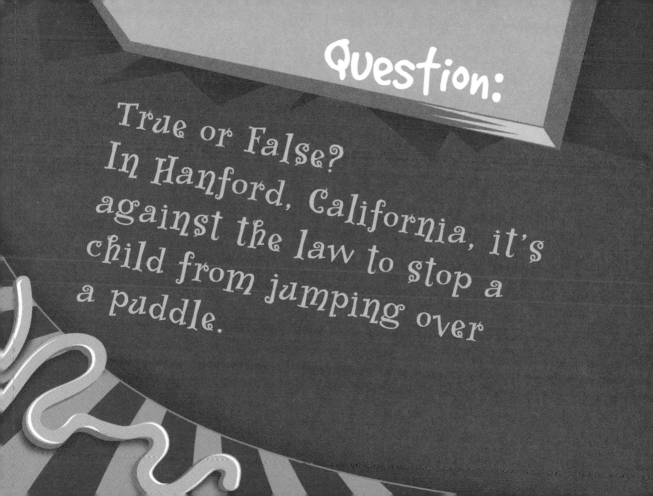

Question:

True or False?
In Hanford, California, it's against the law to stop a child from jumping over a puddle.

Answer:

True! So if you're ever in Hanford and see a good puddle, jump away!

Question:

They don't make $1,000 bills anymore, but if you were lucky enough to find an old one on the sidewalk, which president's picture would be on it? Andrew Jackson? Grover Cleveland? Or Ulysses S. Grant?

Answer:

You'd see a picture of Grover Cleveland, the 22nd and 24th president of the United States.

Goliath from the Bible was a giant of a man—but just how tall was he? Here's a hint: Goliath was taller than any professional basketball player living today.

Goliath was over nine feet tall! You can read all about him in 1 Samuel 17:4.

Question:

Camels are great desert travelers. Do you know why? Is it because they can close their ears and noses to keep out blowing sand? Because they can go a week without a single drink of water? Because they have two rows of eyelashes to protect their eyes? Or because they can carry up to 1,000 pounds?

The answer is . . . Yes! Camels can do all of these things, making them perfectly suited for traveling long distances across a desert!

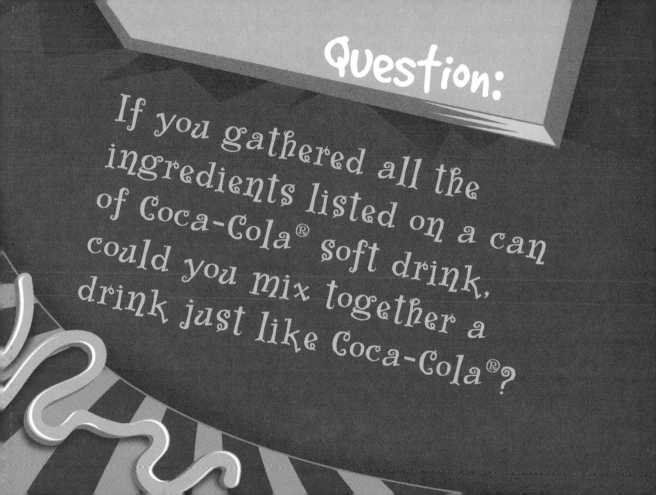

Answer:

The answer is no! That's because there's one secret ingredient not listed on any can of Coca-Cola®. It's called 7X, and only two people in the whole Coca-Cola® company know what it is!

Question:

In Matthew 14:22-33 the Bible tells us that Jesus walked on water—but Jesus wasn't the only person in the Bible who walked on water. Who else did? Here's a hint: It was one of Jesus' followers.

Answer:

Simon Peter was the follower of Jesus who also walked on water. But when Peter took his eyes off Jesus, he became afraid and started to sink! Jesus had to rescue him after all. You can read about it in Matthew 14:29.

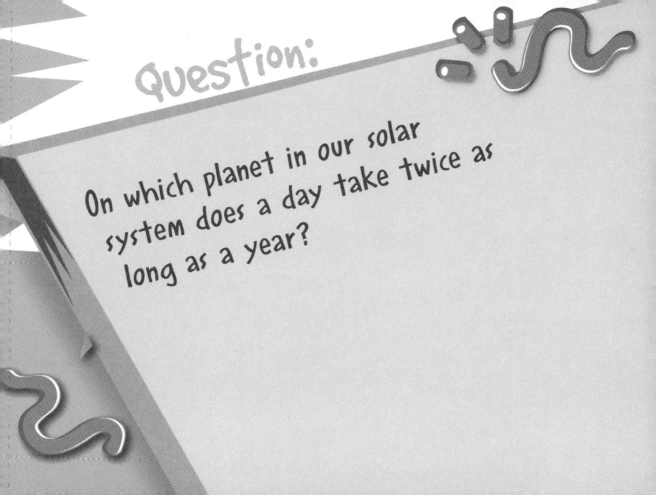

Question:

On which planet in our solar system does a day take twice as long as a year?

On Mercury! Now this can be confusing, so pay attention! It takes Mercury 2,112 hours to travel in its orbit around the sun. That's one "year" for Mercury. But 4,226 hours go by before the planet completes one full "day." That means two years pass on Mercury before one day ends on the same planet!

Question:

The sundew plant sparkles with liquid droplets—but insects attracted to that sparkling better beware! Why?

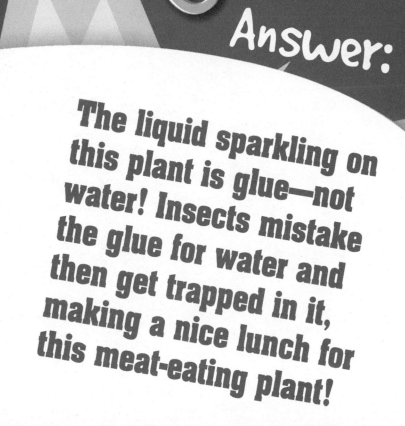

The liquid sparkling on this plant is glue—not water! Insects mistake the glue for water and then get trapped in it, making a nice lunch for this meat-eating plant!

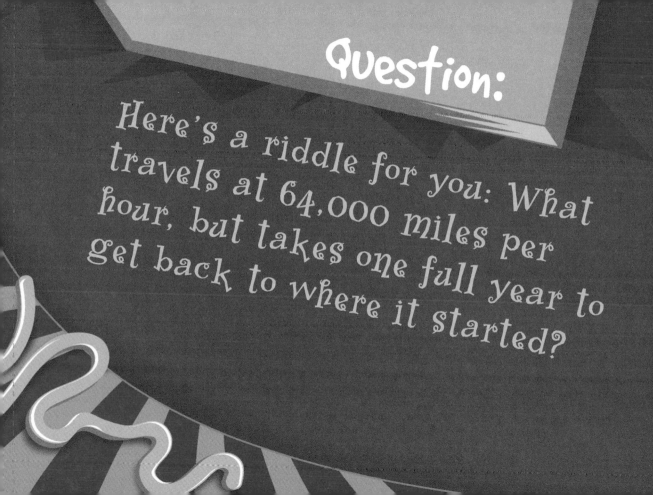

Question:

Here's a riddle for you: What travels at 64,000 miles per hour, but takes one full year to get back to where it started?

Answer:

The Earth! It speeds along at 17 ½ miles per second in its orbit around the sun, taking 365 ¼ days to complete one round-trip through the galaxy.

Question:

Who am I? I was a follower of God during the time of Moses. My donkey actually spoke to me when he saw an angel with a flaming sword! What's my name?

Answer:

Balaam! You can read about my story in Numbers 22:21-35 in the Bible.

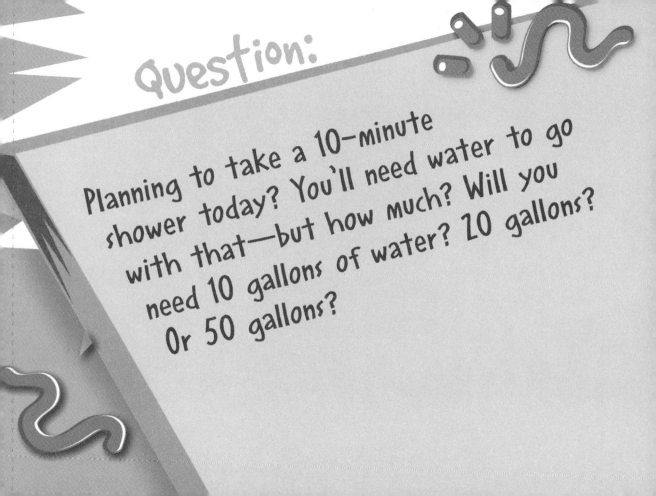

Question:

Planning to take a 10-minute shower today? You'll need water to go with that—but how much? Will you need 10 gallons of water? 20 gallons? Or 50 gallons?

On average, a new showerhead pumps out about five gallons of water per minute, so you'll need around 50 gallons of water for a 10-minute shower today!

Question:

Why do people say "Amen" to end a prayer? Is it because that word means "The end"? "I agree"? Or "Time to open your eyes"?

We say "Amen" because it means "I agree" or "Let it happen." It's our way of telling God we agree with the prayer that was prayed and asking him to answer that prayer. So don't be afraid to say "Amen!" the next time someone you know prays!

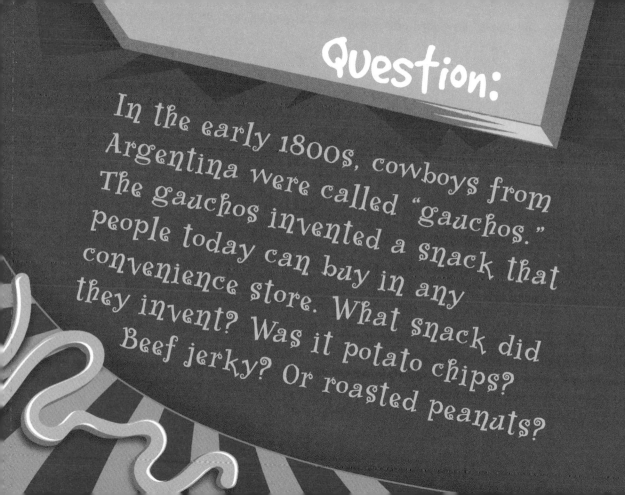

Question:

In the early 1800s, cowboys from Argentina were called "gauchos." The gauchos invented a snack that people today can buy in any convenience store. What snack did they invent? Was it potato chips? Beef jerky? Or roasted peanuts?

Answer:

Gauchos invented beef jerky! They put strips of raw meat under their saddles in the mornings. By the end of the day's ride, the heat and rubbing of their saddles had tenderized and cooked the meat. They called it "charqui," which we now say as "jerky"!

Question:

How many tons of food will you eat in your lifetime? Here's a hint: It's more tons than an average elephant weighs (six tons), but fewer tons than six elephants weigh (36 tons). What's your answer?

Answer:

The average American will eat about 30 tons of food in a lifetime— roughly the weight of five full-grown elephants!

Question:

Chances are you've heard the word "Hallelujah" or even sung it in a song. But what does that word mean? Is it "Praise God"? "He is God"? Or "Sing God's name"?

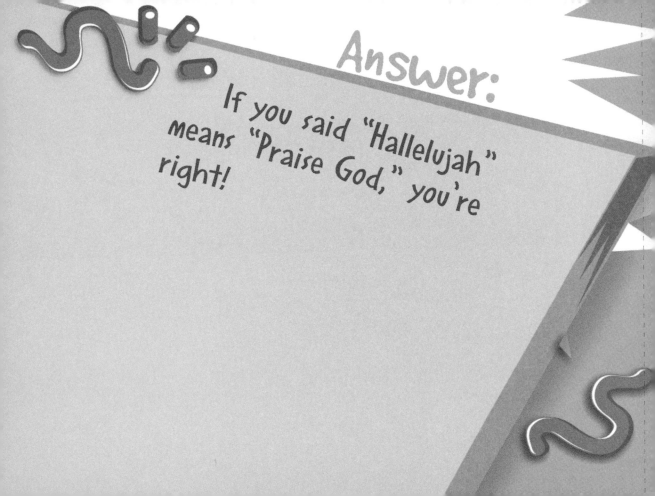

Answer:

If you said "Hallelujah" means "Praise God," you're right!

Question:

If you were a frog, you'd have to take a good look before you jumped from lily pad to lily pad. Do you know why?

Question:

Pop quiz! What are the top three flavors of ice cream in the USA? Ask your friends to help you decide, then see if you are right.

Answer:

The top three flavors are vanilla, chocolate, and Neapolitan (which is actually a combination of vanilla, chocolate, and strawberry).

Question:

John 1:40-42 in the Bible tells us that Andrew, one of Jesus' followers, brought his brother to meet Jesus. Do you know who Andrew's brother was? Here's a hint: It was John, Simon Peter, or James.

Answer:

Andrew's brother was Simon Peter. Peter joined Andrew in following Jesus, and is now known as one of Jesus' most faithful disciples. Just think what might have happened if Andrew hadn't told his brother about Jesus!

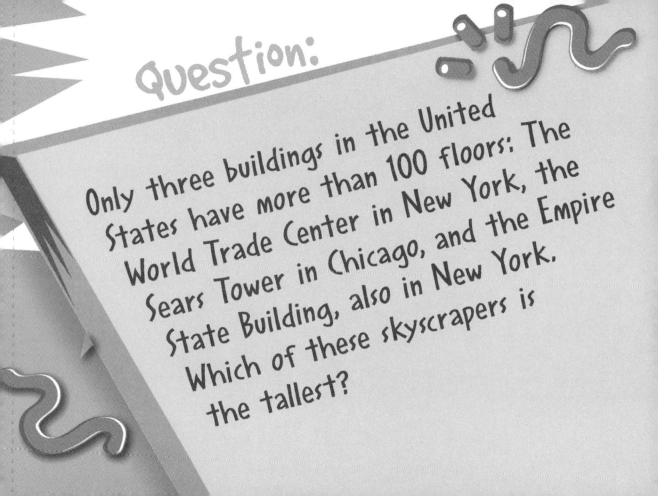

Question:

Only three buildings in the United States have more than 100 floors: The World Trade Center in New York, the Sears Tower in Chicago, and the Empire State Building, also in New York. Which of these skyscrapers is the tallest?

Answer:

With 110 floors, the Sears Tower in Chicago is the tallest building in the USA! The World Trade Center also has 110 floors, but measures about 100 feet shorter than the Sears Tower. The Empire State Building has 102 floors, making it the third-highest building in America. Wow, that's tall!

If you took ten African elephants and stacked them on top of each other, they'd still be shorter than the length of the largest animal in the world. What's the name of that giant animal?

Answer:

The blue whale! This swimming giant can grow to be more than 100 feet long!

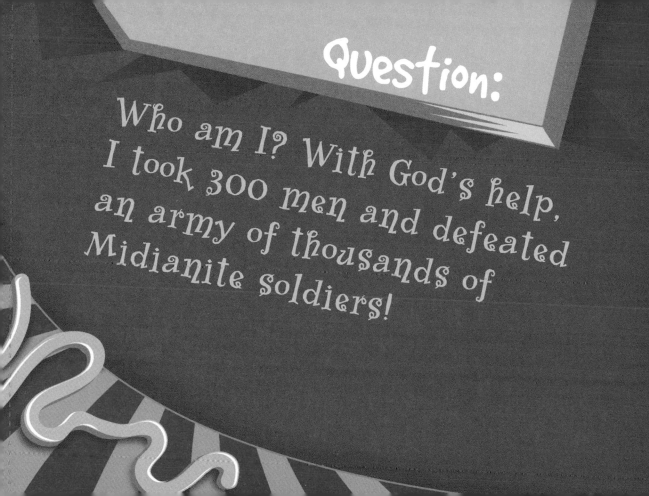

Question:

Who am I? With God's help, I took 300 men and defeated an army of thousands of Midianite soldiers!

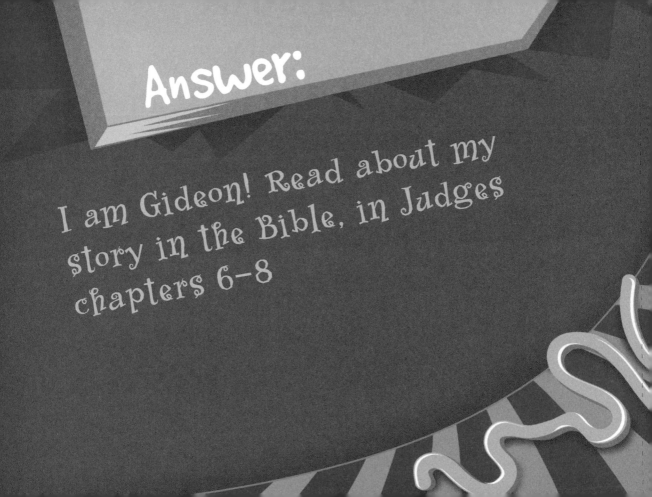

Answer:

I am Gideon! Read about my story in the Bible, in Judges chapters 6-8

Question:

If you're like most kids, you like to eat candy. But how much candy does the average kid eat in a week? Is it one pound? Four pounds? Or six pounds?

Answer:

The average kid eats FOUR POUNDS of candy a week! That's like eating about 40 chocolate bars every week!

Question:

In Denmark they are called "kroner." In Germany they are called "marks." In India they are called "rupees." What are they called in America?

Answer:

Dollars! Kroner, marks, and rupees are all kinds of money.

Question:

Galatians 5:22, 23 in the Bible lists the nine character qualities called "fruit of the Spirit." The first is "love." The second is "joy." What are the rest?

"The fruit of the Spirit is love, joy, peace, patience, kindness, goodness, faithfulness, gentleness, and self-control" Galatians 5:22, 23 (NIV)

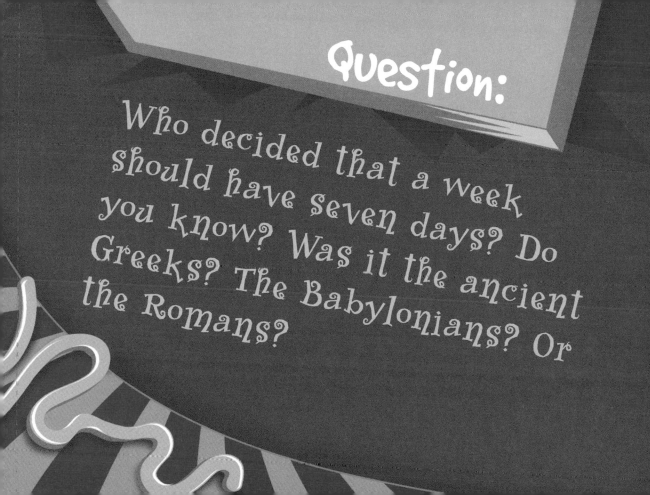

Answer:

Believe it or not, the Greeks used to observe a ten-day week! And the Romans tried a week made up of eight days. The ancient Babylonians, however, noticed that the moon's phases were seven days long, and so they decided to use seven days for a week—and that's what we still use today!

Question:

True or False?
God loves you.
(I know this is an easy
one, but it's
important!)

Answer:

The answer is **TRUE**! If you don't believe it, read these verses from the Bible to find out for yourself: John 3:16; Romans 5:8; and Ephesians 5:2.

Question:

If you wanted to visit the 50th state to join the United States, would you travel to Hawaii? Alaska? Or Arizona?

Answer:

You'd get a plane ticket to the sunny beaches of Hawaii! The Hawaiian Islands became a state in 1960—the last state to join the USA during the twentieth century!

Question:

Which room of your home uses the most water: The kitchen? The laundry room? Or the bathroom?

The bathroom! A typical American bathroom uses about three-fourths (74%) of the total water used in a home. The laundry uses only about one-fifth (21%) of a home's water supply. And the kitchen only requires about one-twentieth (5%) of the family water.

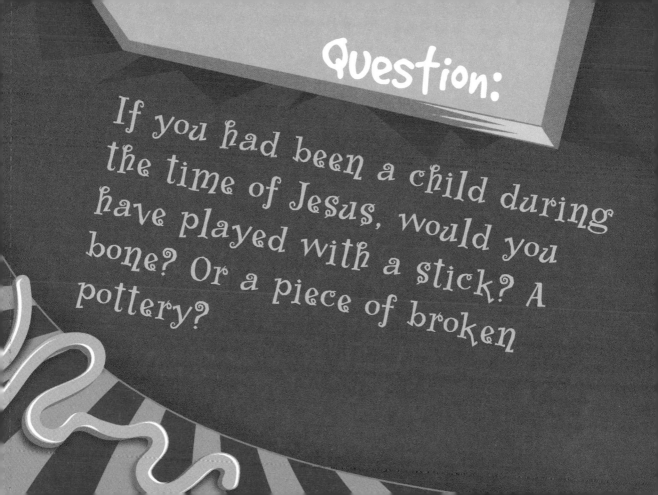

Question:

If you had been a child during the time of Jesus, would you have played with a stick? A bone? Or a piece of broken pottery?

Answer:

You would have played with all those things! Children during that time didn't have many toys, so they used their imaginations and played with things they could easily find laying around—like a stick, a bone or a piece of pottery.

Question:

In Revelation 22:13 in the Bible, Jesus says he is the Alpha and the Omega. Does that mean that he is Greek? That he wants everyone to learn the Greek alphabet? Or that he is the first and last of everything?

Answer:

Alpha and Omega are the first and last letters of the Greek alphabet. So when Jesus tells us that he is "the Alpha and the Omega," that means he is the first and last of everything, the one that makes everything begin and end!

Snickers® and M&M's® are registered trademarks of M&M/MARS, a division of Mars, Inc.

Tootsie Roll® is a registered trademark of Tootsie Roll Industries, Inc.

Coca-Cola® is a registered trademark of the Coca-Cola Company.

Monopoly® is a registered trademark of Hasbro.

Bibliography

Anthony, Susan C. *Facts Plus*. Anchorage: Instructional Resources Company, 1991.

Choron, Sandra and Harry. *The Book of Lists for Kids*. Boston: Houghton Mifflin Company, 1995.

Cosgrove, Ellen. "Fifty Things to Do This Summer," *Sports Illustrated for Kids*, July 1999.

Cosgrove, Ellen and Marlene Rooney. "Kids Ask," *Sports Illustrated for Kids*, July 1999.

Daniels, Patricia, ed. *Amazing Facts*. Alexandria: Time-Life Books, 1994.

Dockrey, Karen and John and Phyllis Godwin. *Holman Student Bible Dictionary*. Nashville: Holman Bible Publishers, 1993.

Doney, Meryl. *How the Bible Came to Us*. Oxford: Lion Publishing, 1985.

Elwood, Ann and Carol Orsag Madigan. *The Macmillan Book of Fascinating Facts*. New York: Macmillan Publishing Company, 1989.

Hill, Nancy S. *Actual Factuals*. Wheaton: Tyndale House Publishers, 1997.

Israel, Elaine, ed. *The World Almanac for Kids 1999*. Mahwah: World Almanac Books, 1998.

Kramer, Ann. *The Random House Children's Encyclopedia*. New York: Random House, 1991.

Martins, Robyn. *Fun Facts About the Bible You Never Knew*. Uhrichsville: Barbour Publishing, Inc., 1996.

Nussbaum, Hedda. *Charlie Brown's Second Super Book of Questions and Answers*. New York: Random House.

Packer, J.I., Merrill C. Tenney, and William White, Jr. *The Bible Almanac*. Nashville: Thomas Nelson Publishers, 1980.

Pyke, Dr. Magnus. *Weird and Wonderful Science Facts*. New York: Sterling Publishing Co., 1984.

Robbins, Pat, ed. *Far-Out Facts*. Washington D.C.: The National Geographic Society.

———. *More Far-Out Facts*. Washington D.C.: The National Geographic Society, 1982.